E N ~~DO~~

"Here is a very compelling presentation of a difficult journey. This story from the heart is a powerful and compelling book."

—Stephen G. Post, Ph.D.
Professor, School of Medicine,
Case Western Reserve University

"Floyd Fought presents a refreshing and honest description of his and Wilma's pilgrimage through the many challenges of caregiving. It is a story of love, devotion, and faith."

—Bill E. Beckwith, Ph.D.
Author, *Managing Your Memory: Practical*
Solutions for Forgetting

"The Rev. Floyd Fought's story, written with candor and insight, will provide a guideline as to how to cope with the demands and ravages of Alzheimer's. Every family confronting the demands of this illness will profit from this richly creative story."

—Rev. Emerson S. Colaw
Retired bishop, The United Methodist Church

"Because the best ideas often come from family caregivers who are willing to try new things, these lessons, gleaned from Floyd's experiences, are priceless for family caregivers."

—Dotty St. Amand, M.S.W.
Executive Director, Alvin A. Dubin Alzheimer's
Resource Center
Fort Myers, Florida

THE LONG ROAD TO GOODBYE

THE LONG ROAD to GOODBYE

OUR JOURNEY WITH ALZHEIMER'S

Floyd Fought

FLOYD FOUGHT

Pleasant Word
A Division of WINEPRESS PUBLISHING

Pleasant Word (a division of WinePress Publishing, PO Box 428, Enumclaw, WA 98022) functions only as book publisher. As such, the ultimate design, content, editorial accuracy, and views expressed or implied in this work are those of the author.

Unless otherwise noted, all Scriptures are taken from the the *New Revised Standard Version* (nrsv), copyright 1989, Division of Christian Education of the National Council of the Churches of Christ in the United States of America. Used by permission. All rights reserved.

ISBN 13: 978-1-4141-1033-2
ISBN 10: 1-4141-1033-2
Library of Congress Catalog Card Number: 2007904178

DEDICATION

This book is dedicated to our children,
Tim, Dan, Steve, and Marilyn,
whose many phone calls made the burden
lighter and the journey brighter while drawing
our family closer together though separated by
hundreds of miles—Thank you.

TABLE OF CONTENTS

PREFACE:
A NOTE FROM OUR
DAUGHTER

Recently, we moved my mother's piano from our house to my brother's home, where his three-year old daughter has become its official guardian. She makes sure that the wooden cover slips over the keys at night, and she removes the cover in the morning. This is how the piano "sleeps" and wakes up.

Mom's piano has a history. My dad scrimped and saved, then traveled miles to get Mom's piano for her when he was just a poor country preacher and their first child was on the way. It wasn't an inexpensive used upright, but a sleek piece of furniture where Mom could play hymns and classical music and give piano lessons.

The memory that I hold close is that of her lively fingers playing the "wild and wicked" notes of ragtime. She would let loose, giving vent to whatever frustrations had come during her day. And there were many of those days for this mother of four, piano teacher, and pastor's wife all wrapped up in a less-than-five-foot frame.

This book was written by my dad about a time in my mom's life when the piano keys fell silent. He has lived through every word of this book in his own sturdy but tender way.

Mom's journey with Alzheimer's touched a lot of lives. As she descended into the depths of this disease, we all moved into new paths that often defied syncopation. Our feet moved where we did not expect to go. Sometimes, to our surprise, our feet could tap in rhythm to her "offbeat" tune, and we could even dance. But none of us could have known there was any kind of music for this journey had Dad not given careful attention to every ragged note of our Mom's process.

The story of this journey came out of my dad's heart in bits and pieces. At first it was something like an agonized therapy, then it became a series of vignettes that he could share with small groups. Often the response was numerous requests for him to put his stories into written form.

And so he spoke and then wrote, and he honed the stories into not only a book of useful advice but also an inspirational source book as well. It is not easy to write about Alzheimer's. It is not easy to read about it. But in these chapters can be heard the faint stanza and refrain of a syncopated score of loss, grief, and sadness. But then the unexpected offbeat lands on a note of surprise and joy. Let yourself feel the offbeat. You might recognize that although it is about a devastating disease, the words, the notes, the rhythm, even the offbeat, all come together as a love story.

This story is my mother's story and my dad's story, written about hope that can be found in love. While it is true that love cannot conquer every mountain, hope can still be found in the hills and valleys of a journey with Alzheimer's. It is this extraordinary love story that buoyed him up in currents of despair that often threatened to pull him under.

Alzheimer's robbed my mother of her memories. This book steals a little bit back from that ruthless thief as, in these vignettes, our memories of her live on.

Marilyn Morris

ACKNOWLEDGEMENTS

I want to offer a special word of thanks to Roger Palms, whose editorial skill organized my writings about our journey with Alzheimer's and gave birth to this book.

INTRODUCTION

In 1904, a woman died in Germany. Her physician was Dr. Alois Alzheimer. Early in his research Dr. Alzheimer had asked the woman, "What is your name?"

"Auguste," she answered.

He asked, "What is your last name?"

"Auguste," came her reply.

"What is your husband's name?"

"Auguste, I think."

So Dr. Alzheimer asked her to write her name and gave her a pen. After a few tries, Frau Auguste D. put down the pen and said softly, "I have lost myself."

Back then the average life span was about forty-seven years. Today, the fastest growing age group is eighty-five and up, when the risk of developing

Alzheimer's or some form of dementia is almost 50 percent. According to one poll taken in 2006, one of the greatest fears of Americans is the fear of losing their mental capacity.

We are afraid of losing ourselves.

Chapter 1

The "A" Word; Welcome to the World of Alzheimer's

Retirement came after nearly fifty years of ministry in the United Methodist Church. My wife, Wilma, and I were thrilled to move into our newly renovated home on the shore of Lake Erie. We dreamed of freedom, travel, winters in Florida, and visits with our four children. We had lived full lives, and now it was time to savor the benefits becoming to senior citizens.

We were still beginning to make plans for an exciting future when we visited a doctor in our new location, and he went over the files sent by our previous physician. He rocked us with the news that he suspected that Wilma was in the very early stages of Alzheimer's. What was he talking about? I knew nothing about the disease. I didn't even know how to spell it. And certainly we had no idea of the implications in the doctor's announcement.

We were referred to a neurologist who confirmed the diagnosis. It was July of 1991, one month after we had retired. Having lived all our married lives in parsonages owned by the church congregations, we had just moved into the first house that we had ever owned and were anticipating the wonderful years ahead. Our journey into a happy future was suddenly thrown into confusion and chaos.

How was it that such a monstrous life-changing disease could suddenly appear out of nowhere? There was no warning pain, no unexplained illness, no dizziness or unsteadiness.

No Idea What Lay Ahead

Our first reaction was denial, followed by unbelief, and then anger. Gradually, denial was replaced by reality, unbelief was set aside by acceptance, and the anger subsided. For me, each of those steps took time, as I not only absorbed the news intellectually but also worked through its emotional impact. But neither Wilma nor I had any idea of what lay ahead of us over the next nine years.

After the diagnosis, we were referred to a neurologist who specialized in the treatment of Alzheimer's; he arranged for an MRI, an EEG, a carotid artery exam, and an appointment with a psychologist. Although Wilma was showing few outward manifestations of the disease, the end result of all the tests confirmed that Wilma was in the beginning stages of Alzheimer's. We made an appointment with the

regional memory clinic to determine the level of
Wilma's Alzheimer's and received their recommen-
dation for appropriate management.

We were at the beginning of this degenerative,
debilitating disease that robs its victims of every skill
and ability, until there is nothing left but a breathing, noncomprehending, noncommunicating shell
of a human being.

Most articles, journals, and books written about
Alzheimer's describe the three stages of the disease
as "early," "middle," and "late." Each stage is then
descried in general terms.

From my personal experience and conversa-
tions with many others, I believe that there is yet
another stage, which I choose to call the "suspicion"
stage. Webster defines suspicion as "an instance of
suspecting something wrong without proof or on
slight evidence." This describes what appears to
me in hindsight to have been our situation during
several years prior to the diagnosis of "early stage
Alzheimer's."

At this early stage of Alzheimer's, the small
changes in Wilma's personality, ability, or skill
were almost imperceptible. Later on, several friends
commented on Wilma's occasional out-of-character
responses, such as a total lack of recall of a shared
event in their lives. For them, this was a suspicion
stage. Something different was occurring but what
and why was unknown and often unspoken.

Wilma May Have Guessed

I now believe that Wilma may have been the first to suspect her illness, but she remained silent in her denial. She would leave her purse or pocketbook at various places. On one occasion, she left her pocketbook on the roof of the car after filling the tank with gas. It flew off as she sped down the road on her way home. We would have never found it had not a kind and honest man seen it fly off the roof of the car. He stopped by the roadside and called us so that we could retrieve it, contents intact. Another time, while traveling, she left her purse in a restaurant. We were already 200 miles down the road when we called the restaurant to ask if it was still there. A Greyhound bus delivered it to our city of destination the next day.

Leaving her purse became such a regular occurrence that it became a part of family humor. It became my responsibility to always make certain that her purse was with us as we prepared for departure.

Although they should have, these and other events like them did not raise suspicion in me about any link to disease. During our married life, Wilma had always managed our financial affairs, written most of the checks, balanced our accounts, and prepared our income tax returns. Then one day she told me that she would no longer handle the checkbook. "Fair enough," I thought; it was now my turn. So I took over writing the checks but found it impossible to figure out the balance.

The "A" Word; Welcome to the World of Alzheimer's

Finally, I called the bank to establish the balance and discovered that our account was several hundred dollars off, in our favor. Looking back, I now realize I should have suspected that something wasn't quite right.

There are other painful recollections of this stage. I recall when long-standing relationships became difficult for Wilma. We had formed a group of friends from college, seminary, and early ministry and had managed to stay together over the next several decades. We met several times a year in each other's homes for meals, games, shoptalk, and lots of laughter. We shared stories of births, graduations, marriages, ministry transfers, career changes, and retirement plans.

For many years, we had enjoyed these special get-togethers with friends. But then Wilma began to fret over the preparations for the next gathering. Afterward, she would tell me emphatically, "I am not going again." When it came time for the next meeting, I made all of the arrangements. But as time went on, I found that I needed to push Wilma harder and harder. With enough persuasion on my part, and perhaps the hope that this time would be different, she would agree to go. At the end it was the same result. She found it increasingly difficult to be with the people and didn't want to return the next time.

I can only surmise what her thinking must have been like. Over the years, our shared experiences became memories that we referenced with just a

23

simple phrase or even a word. When the reference occurred, we would burst out laughing. Now, Wilma could no longer attach the reference to the memory. An increasing fog had obscured it. Since she could no longer laugh with our friends, she either felt left out or, worse, began to believe that they were laughing at her. In retrospect, I regret the pain it must have caused her.

Wilma may have started to become suspicious when she had the incidents with her purse or the checkbook. But those things are not necessarily the forerunners of Alzheimer's. However, the combination of these events may be reason enough to at least start to wonder about changes and ask the family doctor for an opinion.

In days gone by, families and victims of this disease tended to suffer in silence. Today, it is far more likely to be discussed. Since the openness of President Ronald Reagan about his diagnosis of Alzheimer's, magazine and newspaper articles have opened our lips and allowed the "A" word to be spoken more openly. It is now easier for us to raise our suspicions when there are subtle or not-so-subtle changes in performance levels, thought processes, or social contacts. It is much easier to talk about Alzheimer's in ordinary conversation.

The Beginning of Another Kind of Journey

When I first heard our doctor say, "Onset of Alzheimer's," I did not understand the implications of what that meant. As unprepared as we were when we first heard that diagnosis, it triggered the urgent need to make many necessary adjustments for the remaining days of our lives together. It was the end of our dreams for a long, bright, and happy retirement. It was the beginning of another kind of journey that brought us, as a couple and as a family, together in what we had neither planned for nor imagined.

Our journey with Alzheimer's was just beginning. There would be peaks, and there would be valleys. Along the way our journey brought some surprising miracles. In the months and years ahead, I would witness the destruction of everything that was the "apple of my eye" when I met Wilma in 1943. An excellent cook, she would come to a time when she could no longer follow a recipe. This person who had graduated from college with honors, who possessed a brilliant mind, was no longer able to print her own name. I watched this gifted pianist and piano teacher decline until she could not even manage a simple scale. Once she made excellent clothing choices; the day would come when she was at a total loss as to what to wear.

As the disease progressed, routine activities such as bathing, toilet functions, and coherent conversation left. In the early years of the disease, food preparation was a joint effort. But as time went on and Wilma lost her ability to prepare meals, the task became totally mine. We were spared one particular problem of turning the knobs on the kitchen stove, for when the ability to prepare food ceased to exist, it seemed the entire process was lost and would never be recalled.

I watched a proud and independent woman decline to the point where she was confined to a wheelchair, with every bit of food placed on her tongue for her and every drop of liquid brought to her lips by someone other than herself. I watched a private person come to the point of requiring me or, on occasion, someone else to attend to her toilet needs and personal care.

Perhaps the most painful experience came one day when she could no longer recognize her children. It would be as though the person I married in 1946 no longer existed.

Fighting an Incoming Tide

We were often so bewildered. "What's happening?" we would ask over and over again. And, as the losses of Wilma's memory and skills mounted, anger would erupt and boil over into rage. We fought against the encroachment of Alzheimer's, but to no avail. We might as well have fought against the incoming tide.

One night, well into Wilma's years with Alzheimer's, we were walking on the streets near our Ohio lakeside home. A single light at each intersection provided the only illumination. Our elongated shadows followed us as we approached the light and became shorter as we neared the corner. Then as we moved on, our shadows were in front of us.

THE "A" WORD; WELCOME TO THE WORLD OF ALZHEIMER'S

The poem of Robert Louis Stevenson came to mind. "I have a little shadow/ that goes in an out with me. And what can be the use of him/is more than I can see." Those words became hauntingly real as I made the connection between our walk in the night and our walk with Alzheimer's. I could not escape Wilma's presence. It was as if we were mysteriously connected. Everywhere I went, she wanted to be there with me. Sometimes, when I went to another room, she would follow silently, for no other reason than just to be there.

I realized that when everything else had left her, she was determined that I was not to leave her. The persistence of this constant presence developed an unbelievable bond between us. It was a bond beyond words, since her speech pattern was by then destroyed. It was a bond beyond the physical and in the realm of the spiritual. In our marriage, two very different personalities had become one. But it took nine years with Alzheimer's to ripen even more the love that had started fifty-seven years before.

For yet there was joy—a strange word to describe my emotions at a time like this. The apostle Peter wrote of "an indescribable joy" (see 1 Peter 1:8). An Old Testament writer said that there was a time for everything (see Ecclesiastes chapter 3). For us, there had been a time of shock, a time of bewilderment, a time of confusion, a time of loss, a time of sorrow. But God knows what time it is for each of us. Jesus said that if a sparrow falls from the sky, God knows.

FOR FURTHER THOUGHT...

Illness is usually detected by body talk, i.e., pain, fever, upset stomach, etc., sending us to the doctor for analysis. But Alzheimer's didn't come to us that way. I can see hints of the illness with 20/20 hindsight that I didn't see at the time. Subtle personality changes, incidents of mental disconnect were there, but I didn't see them then.

That's why it is so important to have a diagnosis as early as possible. I told the physician who made the initial diagnosis that I considered him to be one of my very best friends, because he honestly followed his suspicions in determining his diagnosis. Difficult as it may be and harsh as it may appear, it is my opinion that everyone involved is better served by receiving diagnoses as early as possible and therefore give the family more time to begin to adjust to what is coming.

Medical science is making significant strides, and appropriate treatment can at least improve the quality of life. Early diagnosis can start those treatments. And, of course, it gives the Alzheimer's patient and his or her loved ones time to discuss and plan and think through their future.

Chapter 2

· ·

THE BEST DAY
POSSIBLE FOR WILMA

The fog comes on little cat feet." So begins a poem by Carl Sandburg. And like fog, so does Alzheimer's. It comes so quietly that by the time the doctor defines the cause of the noticed difficulty, the patient has already started down the path of this disease.

During our early years with Alzheimer's, very few things changed; the effects of the disease were hardly noticeable. But the middle years, perhaps three to six years into the disease, brought significant changes.

The doctor had told us early on that Wilma should not drive. One day, in the doctor's office, I was going through my wallet, discarding outdated cards, and was shocked to see that my driver's license had expired. When I looked at Wilma's license, it was one year past expiration.

In my preoccupation with caring for Wilma, I had failed to keep up with this detail. When I checked with the licensing bureau, I learned that I could have my license renewed, because it was only one month past due. But Wilma's license was a year old. She would need to take a driving test.

I got the book to help Wilma study by reading the questions and the answers aloud and even writing down the answers. But it was obvious that her memory system was already in decline.

The day of the examination is still painful to me. Wilma was given the questions and instructed to sit on the opposite side of the room from me. Other applicants came, wrote out their answers, and left to take their road test. Wilma was still struggling with her answers.

Finally, she took her papers to the officer. She passed the written test and was sent outside for the driving test. But she failed the parallel parking, knocking down the cones. So she was told to go home and practice and come back for another test.

After we returned home, I made some makeshift cones for practice. We went to a remote area and set up the cones. But I could see that it was impossible for her to execute the parallel parking concept. Parallel parking requires a series of judgments and decisions that make it difficult for many, and for Wilma, it was impossible. After many hours of trying, we decided to delay the attempt to get a license.

Later she did try again and failed to pass the driving test. She was devastated; it was a terrible blow to her psyche. On the way home, I tried to make the best of the situation, stating that since I was retired, I could be chauffeur. We talked about her close friend who was the mother of three, active in church and community affairs, and operated a children's day care in her home. But she never learned how to drive a car. I said that we really didn't need to pursue a license. In the silence that followed, there appeared to be acceptance, because the loss of a driver's license was never talked about for the rest of her life.

Wilma had never had a traffic accident, and now we were shielded from possible accident because of an error in judgment. There are numerous stories in the Alzheimer's community of people who were still driving and were found miles from home, confused about how to return. The speed and number of cars on our highways leaves us with almost zero tolerance for any person with impaired judgment. For Wilma, it was a defeat, a loss of independence. But, at the same time, it was best.

Wilma found that she was no longer able to manipulate the dials on our washer and dryer. Playing the piano had been one of her favorite pastimes, but gradually that became impossible. As the disease progressed, routine activities such as bathing, dressing, and coherent conversation left her.

A World Real to Her

I felt guided by one principle: I would do anything and everything to make each day the best possible day for Wilma. From our more than fifty years together, I knew what she did and did not like. I knew the little personal stories that brought a smile or a frown. As time passed and the disease progressed, I was able to refine my ability to cope, emphasizing the positive and avoiding unpleasantness. I tried to function based on the assumption that Wilma's world was real to her, regardless of how absurd it might seem to me. When there were delusions, I found it best to respond as if the delusions were real and move on to some diversion. I was not always successful, but it was easier than arguing about the delusion.

Our days took on the characteristics of both of our lives. She was an early riser and thus, early to bed. I had difficulty getting up and equal difficulty sleeping at night. Our day now started when Wilma awakened, sometimes as early as 4:00 A.M. It was a major adjustment for me, but I came to enjoy the sunrises and the awakening songs of the birds.

Keeping Regular Routines

Our morning ritual started when Wilma started. This included breakfast, bathing, dressing, and a moderate amount of house cleaning. I was learning how to care for her through trial and error, reading any article I could find, going to numerous seminars, and participating in a local support group. With the passing years, each task with Wilma took longer to accomplish. In the latter stages of the disease, my entire day was spent caring for Wilma.

THE BEST DAY POSSIBLE FOR WILMA

When her life-long problem of irregular bowel movements was exacerbated by her medications, loss of appetite, and general lack of activity, a nurse suggested that an eight-ounce glass of warm prune juice with pulp would help her. Thus, every day started with prune juice and her usual morning medicines. I learned that it was important for me to follow this routine before proceeding further. The microwave oven proved helpful, because I could prepare our oatmeal without burning it. Before the microwave, I was forever allowing the oatmeal to boil over or burn in the pan.

In the early years, Wilma could feed herself. But soon it became necessary for me to feed her. I spent many hours with this procedure. In later years it would take one to two hours for her to drink the prune juice and eat the oatmeal. Breakfast and cleanup consumed a lot of time, often most of the morning. I tried to keep reminding myself that I was retired, and there was nothing else that I really had to do.

In the beginning, Wilma regulated her own toilet times, but in the later years, it became my responsibility to monitor that activity. As a result, incontinence was delayed until the last year of her life. Eventually, I had to seek professional advice when I was faced with the need to administer an enema.

As time passed, the morning routine often stretched to noon or beyond. If it took an hour or two to feed Wilma a bowl of oatmeal, I was content. I knew no institution would take that kind of time. I was reminded of the story found in Matthew 25:31-46, where the King, Father, God blessed those who were least in his family. The long time spent in feeding Wilma became a rich blessing to me.

At first, we tried to watch television during the feeding time, but the rapid movement of images seemed to aggravate her. Finally it became obvious that some scenes, especially scenes of violence, whether in a newscast or film story, upset her. This was the opposite of what she might have experienced in an institution, where TV often serves as a "babysitter." It gave added validity to my determination to delay as long as possible, or even avoid altogether, institutional care.

When the kitchen was cleaned and the bed made, we often had a relaxing time when we could listen to music—classic, pop, or hymns. I became a big fan of Karl Haas on PBS, from whom I learned a great deal about classical music. I gained a greater appreciation for the music and the masters who produced it.

I scheduled all doctor appointments, hospice nurse calls, and any errands that involved Wilma, in the late morning or early afternoon. While she was unable to control events around her, I was able to provide some regularity. Both from my reading and experience, I knew that this was particularly beneficial. Midday was snack and siesta time. When Wilma's appetite left her, or when breakfast stretched to almost noon, I often gave her a glass of a vitamin-fortified drink or a milkshake fortified with bananas or other fruit.

Our afternoon activity was often determined by the morning's events. When weather permitted, we liked to walk. This gave us time out of the house, fresh air, and brief moments of social contacts with the people we met. Sometimes we took a short drive to visit with family or friends. Occasionally, we would stop at a restaurant for a late afternoon meal. Since I never knew if Wilma would eat, I would order one meal that I knew she would enjoy and feed her as much as she would eat. If she ate most or all of the meal, I would order dessert or raid the refrigerator when we got home. Generally one meal was sufficient for both of us.

On most days, the evening meal was next on our agenda. My prior experience in the kitchen had been limited to carving the Thanksgiving turkey. When the routine measuring and preparing of the food became first difficult and then impossible for Wilma, I had to become the cook. By seeking advice from friends and family, as well as reading cookbooks, I developed a series of menus that enabled me to prepare a grocery list that would carry us through as much as two weeks. The television cooking programs were quite helpful to me with their how-to-do-it demonstrations. To my surprise, planning and preparing the evening meal became a pleasure.

The late afternoons and early evening mealtime became almost a sacred time for us. The time spent in preparation and eating became special. In our early years, I was merely the kitchen help, but my role changed when I was forced to become the main cook.

When Wilma lost her ability to use a knife and fork, I had to cut all her food into bite-sized pieces and feed her. When chewing became a problem for her, I sought advice and learned that the answer to eating most foods was simply to puree them. I bought a small food processor and incorporated pureeing into the meal preparation time. Our evening meal could require two or more hours; however, this was also the best time of the day. There was close eye contact, and I never allowed the phone to interrupt us.

The Avoidance of "Sundowning"

After dinner, it was time to get ready for bed. I was always hopeful that the relaxing pace of mealtime had prepared Wilma for sleep, and we would avoid *sundowning*. "Sundowning" is a common problem for Alzheimer's patients who become more irritable, agitated, or even aggressive in the late afternoon as the sun goes down. We avoided the "sundowning" problem by following the same routine each day and avoiding any stimulus such as caffeine, sugar, TV, or evening activities. It was time for brushing teeth, a routine ability that Wilma slowly lost. I tried to follow a bedtime routine much as she had done with the children years before— washing hands and face, one more potty time, and changing into sleep clothes.

Bedtime often provided a special time of conversation or, when possible, the reading of a short devotional. For many months, I would sing some of the familiar gospel songs. Memorization was never one of my strengths, but a friend gave me a song-book containing many traditional hymns. It was a wonderful way to close our day—by lying on the bed together while I sang to her. Sometimes, by midway through the second verse of a song, I could tell by her breathing that Wilma was asleep.

After a few minutes, I would get out of bed and go into the living room for my personal time of the day. It was usually the only time I was free from the care of Wilma. I could read or watch television. I bought an attachment that permitted me to hear the TV sound through a set of headphones.

I could even go for short walks. Hospice had provided me with a gadget similar to those placed in a baby's room that detected motion and alerted parents in another part of the house. I found that it worked for several hundred feet, so I placed it beside her in the bed and went outside for a walk. I would take a path that kept me close to the moni-tor. This personal freedom contributed greatly to my emotional and physical health for the duration of Wilma's illness.

Wandering at Night

There was one potential problem that came at night. Alzheimer's patients may wander about dur-ing the night. Professionals have several theories as to the cause, but I can only describe how I dealt with it. When Wilma first began wandering at night, she would just walk and walk throughout the apartment. If I got her back into bed, she just got up and started walking again. This could continue for hours, which made sleep impossible for me.

Rules in our retirement community prevented securing the door with inside locks, so for a time, I placed a blanket at the exit door and tried to sleep on the floor next to the door. Finally, my resolution to the problem had unexpected benefits. When it was obvious that the walking was going to continue, I would get dressed, dress Wilma, and we would both go for a walk—regardless of the hour. I found it to be a wonderful adventure when we set out on our trek during the night. I determined to walk until I could sense that Wilma was worn out and would be ready for sleep.

The night walks provided a variety of sounds and sights not experienced in the daytime. Crickets and tree frogs sing their songs only at night. Some animals are nocturnal and are seen mostly at night. One night, a mother skunk, followed by her four babies, amused Wilma. Another night, a raccoon chattered at us, and a rabbit hopped playfully in front of us. Occasionally a dolphin would swim along the sea wall next to the sidewalk, or a night heron would stand on the wall waiting for its next meal. Animals seem to have less fear of humans at night.

In the dim light of night, we saw everything in black and white. Every night became a three-dimensional Ansel Adams' photo. All of this, plus the millions of stars above, made our venture into the night something to anticipate rather than something to despise. The long walks proved to be an excellent option to an otherwise dreadful situation and once again provided an experience that was beyond the ability of an institution to provide.

Taking My Mind off of the Struggles

Battling isolation was a persistent problem for me. I'm a people person by nature, but also because of my life as a pastor. I found several ways to combat the sense of isolation. One of the best ways was to use the telephone to visit neighbors, friends, and family. I used these calls to replay the events of the day or discuss topics on my mind. I found television, especially travel programs, to be a wonderful escape. Anything I could do to take my mind off of the struggles of the day was a healthy exercise.

I tried to vary how I used my free time, but I *always* kept the same daily routine for Wilma. I knew that with her there was the constant possibility of sudden change with no rational explanation. This meant that I always had to be ready to alter our daily plan to fit the situation. While there was no typical day, there was the one consistent objective; I was going to do anything and everything to make this day the best possible day for Wilma.

FOR FURTHER THOUGHT...

A friend, Don Yaussy, was dealing with his wife's Parkinson's disease. She was requiring care twenty-four hours a day. In a letter to me he wrote: "I was at sixes and sevens with myself. I wanted to do this. I wished I could do that, and I was torn with inner conflict until I decided to make Phyllis my sole priority." I knew that this would also be one of my guiding principles during Wilma's remaining days of life.

Don's challenge, coupled with particular verses of Scripture, became powerful gifts for the journey: "Let us lay aside every weight and run with perseverance the race that is set before us" (Hebrews 12:1); "I have learned in whatever state I am to be content" (Philippians 4:11); "I can do all things through him [Christ] who strengthens me" (Philippians 4:13).

These were words that I could hold on to, words that even in my deepest and darkest times brought comfort and strength. I never had doubts, but sometimes, when I was in despair, I felt very lonely. God strengthened me to do the task of loving Wilma even at the most difficult times in her life, which I realized were the most difficult times for me as well.

Chapter 3

. . . .

THE POWER OF
CHOICE

C hoose this day whom you will serve" (Joshua 24:15). These words from the Old Testament Scripture took on new meaning for me during our journey with Alzheimer's. I came to understand that the gift of choice sets people apart from all the other creatures. Therefore, I felt that to exercise my freedom of choice in the manner of care I was to give my wife was for me the fullest expression of my humanity.

Living with Wilma's Alzheimer's gave me an opportunity to experience the unbelievable power of choice. As the ravages of the disease took their toll, I saw Wilma's opportunity for personal choice diminished. In contrast, I became more aware of the fantastic gift of choice that was mine.

I could choose the type and color of my clothing. I could choose when and what to eat. I could choose where and how I wanted to go. I could choose where I wanted to live. And I could choose to love or hate. I could choose to be angry at my situation or to accept it.

Losing the Ability to Choose

Wilma gradually lost her ability to choose. She couldn't make up her mind what to wear. She would try one dress or outfit and then another, but none were quite appropriate. When there were four or five different outfits spread out on the bed, I would return them to their place in the closet and challenge her. I'd ask, "What are you doing? Why are you doing this?" But she couldn't explain. Soon others would be over the bed or chair or lying here and there. I hung them up, she took them down; the apartment would be a mess, and I was worn out.

Then I chose not to fight it. When she started with the clothing selection routine, I relaxed and let it run its course. Sometimes, before it was over, the closets were empty, and clothing was scattered in every room. She seemed to be content, and then she often fell asleep. Although the apartment was covered with clothing, in fifteen or twenty minutes I could return all the clothes to the closet while she rested. This response was much better. True, the house would be a mess, but so what? She was not destructive in any way. No one was being injured. I chose to relax, read a book, listen to music, or just look out the window.

Early on, I learned that it was important to understand that her world was very different from mine. How she perceived things, how she understood things, was hidden from me. Moreover, she could not change her behavior or the way she faced the situation that surrounded her. In contrast, by choice, I could alter my own thinking and behavior.

Seeing Pink Elephants

A friend, whose wife suffered from a similar dementia, illustrated it for me this way. When his wife saw pink elephants in the middle of the living room, that was the real world for her. No amount of discussion or argument would change her perception. What was the resolution? My friend would change his perception and join her in seeing the pink elephants in the living room. It was not necessary to agree with her all the time, but it was essential to make every effort to understand what it must be like for her and to adjust his own thinking and actions accordingly.

Another interesting problem emerged when Wilma was confronted with a stairway. In her confusion, she lost the process of negotiating one step after another with alternate feet. She was still able to walk, but when we approached a stairway she could not make her feet execute the proper maneuvers. No amount of argument or training was going to change the "world" that she was experiencing. It was necessary to make some changes if we were to continue with our walking.

I discovered that one step did not present a problem so, for example, we could negotiate a street curb. The resolution was to plan our walks to face only street curbs, ramps, or elevators, and not stairs. Sometimes this made for longer walks, which was good exercise and avoided embarrassment and confrontation.

Rafting in Uncharted Waters

It is nearly impossible to list all of the necessary changes a caregiver is called upon to make while caring for a person with Alzheimer's or dementia. Creative imagination is necessary in responding to the changes. Regular attendance at support groups provided me with much needed assistance in learning how to cope with Wilma's limitations.

As I look back over the years of caring for Wilma, I am amazed at the options left to me, often with multiple choices. Central to everything was the choice to care for her, even if it ended up destroying my own life. This kind of decision may not be possible for everyone, but for me it was the right decision. All other choices were guided by this overriding principle.

From my journals, which I kept during Wilma's illness, I saw that three principles resulted from my choices. I had freedom, peace, and security. Under freedom I wrote that I had never felt freer in all of my life. Even though my care for Wilma was 24/7, I was wonderfully free. It was during this time I was reminded of Terry Anderson's book, *Den of Lions*. He wrote the book after being held captive in a seven-by-nine-foot cell for seven years. He was chained to the floor, except for brief toilet breaks and grueling periods of questioning. However, he came to the conclusion that he was the free person and his captors were the ones who were in bondage. I remember thinking, "If Terry Anderson could feel free under those circumstances then I could be free as well." Wilma was trapped in the bondage of Alzheimer's, and there was nothing that I could do to release her. But I was free. I had chosen of my own free will to do what I was doing. I had not only the freedom of choice but also a choice to be free. The exhilaration from that discovery remained with me.

A Volcano of Rage

From a life of activity with people, I was now facing long stretches of time when there was only minimal contact with anyone other than my wife, who was rapidly slipping into oblivion. There were days, long lonely hours, when I felt abandoned. Nothing, it seemed, could erase the sense of isolation I was experiencing.

I could not stop what was happening to Wilma. Years of caring 24/7 had exhausted my physical and emotional reserves. One night, when all around me was darkness and hopelessness, a volcano of rage erupted from somewhere deep within me. I lashed out at the only source I thought should assist me—God. The next minutes were filled with words expressing my thoughts of a God who would leave me in a mess like this.

When it was over, the silence in the room was devastating. What, oh what, had I done? It was then that I heard a voice like no other voice I have ever heard. I cannot describe what it was like. But I know who it was that spoke, "I'm still here with you." I almost laughed out loud. God was not going to leave me over an angry emotional burst.

In my journal I wrote about peace. I had found that in spite of the storm that raged around me, there came a peace that defied description. From a prison cell the writer of Philippians 4:7 tells of a peace that surpasses all understanding. That became my experience. An artist once put on canvas his interpretation of peace by painting a bird sitting on a nest with a storm raging all around. I read the words of Jesus, words to his disciples shortly before his death, "I will not abandon you" (John 4:18). It was music to my spirit.

Rabbi Kushner writes in *The Lord Is My Shepherd* that the heart of the 23rd Psalm is "I fear no evil, for you are with me" (Psalm 23:4). He then quotes from Martin Buber, who explained the difference between theology and religion by saying that theology was *talking about God* while religion was *experiencing God*.

My theology, developed through years of study of the Scriptures and great writers, was deeply satisfying to me. I had expanded my theological understanding by paying attention to all the current theological trends. Fifty years of study and reflection yielded for me a profound understanding about God.

Now this wonderful experience with God became the anchor to my faith. Nothing could happen to Wilma or to me that would or could separate us from God's love, God's presence. Nothing I would say or do could drive him away. He was going to be with me no matter what. "For I am convinced that neither death, nor life, nor angels, nor rulers, nor things present, nor things to come, nor powers, nor height, nor depth, nor anything else in all creation, will be able to separate us from the love of God in Christ Jesus our Lord" (Romans 8:38-39).

I also wrote in my journal about security. I recall writing about how I felt at a certain point in our journey. I wrote: "It is like riding solo on a giant raft, going down a rapidly flowing stream. I can hear the waters going over the rapids, but I cannot see the difficulties ahead. I am in uncharted waters. I have never been this way before. I have no one with me to pilot the raft. I do not know what the future holds, but the greatest miracle is that I do not need to know what is coming. Life is out of control, but more importantly, I do not need to be in control. As a result, I am more secure than at any other time in my life. I choose to surrender the need to control and, in return, I have gained an unbelievable sense of security."

The decision to be a caregiver and to do all in my power to delay, postpone, or avoid institutional care for Wilma gave me the opportunity to see up close the value of choice. Each passing day, I watched someone I loved being robbed of one more part of her humanity. Each day, she was left with one less choice. Her choices were becoming more limited with each passing day, but my choices were limited only by my imagination.

My choice to care for Wilma, no matter what, was made early on in our journey with Alzheimer's. However, I needed sufficient strength to carry me to the end. It was here I found the essential resource in the word "will." When Wilma and I married, I was asked, "Will you love, comfort, honor her and keep her, in sickness and in health, forsaking all others, and be faithful to her as long as you both shall live?" That question was not, "Are you able?" but "Will you?" Once I coupled that "will you" to my decision to care for Wilma, unbelievable power was released.

FOR FURTHER THOUGHT...

Terry Anderson was a journalist, a foreign correspondent living in Lebanon, when he was kidnapped and imprisoned for seven years. During his captivity, he was tortured, enduring both physical and mental anguish. But he thought of himself as free and his captors as the ones in bondage.

Reading Terry Anderson's conclusion about his freedom sent my spirits soaring. I pictured the comparisons and the contrast between his seven-by-nine-foot cell and my apartment. His freedom was restricted by force; my freedom was restricted by choice. I was free, even though by this time my care for Wilma was consuming twenty-four hours of each and every day. I exclaimed to myself these words, "If Terry Anderson can be free and survive in his 'den of lions,' then I can be free as well." It was a moment I will always remember.

Chapter 4

FORTY-EIGHT HOURS A DAY

For the Alzheimer's caregiver, each day is a virtual forty-eight-hour day. I cooked all the meals. I washed all the dishes. I washed all the clothes. I gave the baths, brushed the teeth, combed the hair—for Wilma and for me. Twenty-four hours a day, times two people, equals forty-eight hours a day.

For the last five years of her life, I did everything that was needed about the house and for her. For the last two years, when she could no longer handle a spoon, I fed her. When she could no longer hold a cup, I helped her drink. For the last six months of her life, I changed every soiled diaper so that she was never wet or dirty.

How did I do it? It was not always easy. Sometimes Wilma was very angry; sometimes she wept uncontrollably; sometimes my nerves got frayed. Sometimes I was the one who was weeping. Wilma's decline was steady. Although the progression of each Alzheimer's patient is different, we can generally know that tomorrow will probably not be as good as today.

As I look back over the years, what occurred was like watching a video in reverse and in extra-slow motion. The changes in Wilma were gradual, so coping was also gradual. Just as young parents acquire the ability to care for their newborn, so the caregiver can acquire the skills to manage a person with Alzheimer's.

Change Will Occur

The key word in care giving is "change." In coping with Alzheimer's, the changes may be subtle or traumatic but, in one way or another, change will occur. A physician used the following illustration to describe what is happening in the brain of one who has Alzheimer's. Imagine that there are millions of nerve circuits that carry information to the brain for filing. When the information is needed, it is recovered from the file and appropriately used. With Alzheimer's, the cells which make up the circuits die and hence, the circuit is broken. Therefore a skill is lost, or a fact cannot be retrieved. When the cells die and the circuit is broken, the loss is permanent, and change is inevitable.

So the caregiver must be flexible and ready to change. Since the person with Alzheimer's cannot alter the effects of the disease, everyone with whom the patient is in contact must make the appropriate adjustments. There were a number of ways our lives changed which required flexibility on my part.

Regular routines were necessary for her comfort, but my routines had to change to meet whatever was happening at that moment. For example, Wilma would pull at the buttons on her dress. One beautiful green dress had large buttons down the front. I had to sew at least one button back on each time she wore that dress. Our house was not dusted every Friday as it once was. Our clothes were clean, but they did not always get ironed. What happened each day, and the adjustments needed, were determined by the way the disease was affecting Wilma that day.

For many years we were part of a group that met periodically for food and fellowship. So one day we planned to gather at a popular restaurant for lunch. It was a three-hour drive for us, which meant an early rising. I prepared breakfast, bathed, and dressed Wilma, and we were on our way.

We arrived at the restaurant about the same time as the others and had warm, pleasant greetings in the parking lot. The restaurant was full of customers, except for the table for twelve set up for our party. There was a lot of chatter, and the decibel level was raised by our laughter and conversation. We placed our orders and then settled in for conversation, catching up on the latest news about one another.

Suddenly Wilma became very agitated. Had she misunderstood something that someone said? Did she misread someone's facial expression? Was it the noise in the room? There was nothing I could do to quiet her. The tempest was rising, so I took her to another area, where I tried to calm her. After a few minutes she seemed to be more in control, so we returned to the table. But as soon as we approached our table, the agitation came back with even greater velocity. Because her speech patterns were largely destroyed, it was impossible to discern what was disturbing her. Finally it was obvious that we needed to leave, and we asked our friends to notify the waitress.

Soon we were on our three-hour journey home without having either lunch or the pleasantries of socializing. The tempest was past, but my disappointment was obvious in the silence that prevailed as the miles slipped away. In time, Wilma went to sleep, and we never mentioned what had happened. By this time, so much short-term memory was gone that what happened one minute was gone the next. It was as if the slate was wiped clean, so any kind of reminder was useless. When she would ask the same question for the twentieth time, it was the first time for her. So I had to learn to keep my frustrations in check.

Handling New Fears

My wife had always been subject to claustrophobia, but now it took on new forms. In distance perception, the coordination of the eye and brain enables us to determine the relative distance of objects that are away from us. But when this process has been interrupted by Alzheimer's, all kinds of problems develop. While driving on a four-lane highway, if we were in the left (inside) lane and a car came along on our right side, Wilma immediately became agitated. So I learned to remain in the right lane of traffic which, I discovered, was a more relaxing way of driving.

Another place where distance perception became a problem was in stores, particularly grocery stores. We tried to avoid crowded areas—doctors had told me early on to avoid places like shopping malls—but the checkout lane presented a special problem. Here the lane is enclosed on both sides; carts and people are fore and aft. One day as we approached the narrow lane at the checkout counter, Wilma was in front of the grocery cart, and I was pushing it. Suddenly, Wilma broke out in a tirade against the man who was immediately in front of her. Since by this time, most of her speech pattern had gone, it was impossible to understand what she was saying to him. But her eyes and face displayed her anger. The poor man had done nothing to stir up her anger and was bewildered by it. When I could get between them, the conflict was over. I apologized to this stranger and explained to him the situation.

A few minutes later, while I was signing my grocery ticket, Wilma approached a young woman and started jabbering at her. I rushed to them, fearing a second confrontation, but instead I saw that Wilma wasn't angry but had a pleasant smile. From this and other situations, I saw a pattern developing which usually involved older men. I learned to keep myself between her and men, especially older men, so Wilma wouldn't feel that they were encroaching into her space.

Another situation that required adjustment on my part was with mirrors. Why mirrors created a problem remains unclear. Was it an inability to process the reflection? Did she wonder who was looking at her? Was that person in the mirror invading her space? When Wilma saw her own reflection in the mirror, a quarrel started with "that person" in the mirror. I soon became aware of the many reflecting surfaces we had about the house. I had installed long mirrors on the back of the closet doors. So I had to remove those mirrors or cover them.

The big mirror in our bathroom was a problem. Each time Wilma looked in that mirror, there was a quarrel with the person she saw in the mirror. Yet I needed a mirror for shaving and combing my hair. So I had to make another adjustment. I found a piece of cardboard big enough to cover the mirror. Then I cut a square hole in the cardboard high enough for me to see to shave but too high for Wilma to see her reflection. Later, at my request, three of our grandchildren drew pictures on sheets of paper, and I covered the entire cardboard area. After that, when guests used our bathroom, they returned to the living room with smiles on their faces.

I soon saw that there are hundreds of reflecting surfaces around us that become mirrors, each one a source of serious conflict for Wilma. Most of the time this conflict could be avoided, such as when passing store windows, by walking between Wilma and that reflecting glass. One day, I was assisting Wilma into the passenger seat of our car when suddenly, she began a heated argument with her image in the door window. When she got seated, she wanted to continue the argument, only to discover that her adversary had disappeared. Her face registered her bewilderment, and in spite of the situation, it did provide me with a bit of humor. To avoid this difficulty, I always made sure that I was between her and the car window.

During one phase of Wilma's decline, I intercepted all of her letters and notes. Previously, her handwriting was beautiful, and her spelling was perfect. Now the writing was hardly legible, and the spelling was so poor it was often difficult to understand what she was trying to convey. So I always took the mail to the mailbox so that I could remove her letters. Later, often at night, I opened the envelopes and rewrote the notes with a notation, "edited by Floyd." I continued to do that until she lost all ability and desire to correspond.

Aware of a Huge Emptiness

Occasionally I would find Wilma sitting alone on the couch and sobbing so hard her entire body seemed to be near convulsions. She was never able to explain why she was crying or what had triggered the sorrow. I can only suppose that in a brief moment of lucidity the enormity of all this was in some way clear to her, and no amount of consolation or questions or admonitions would bring her relief. However, in a moment of inspiration that I think must border on the miraculous, I was given the way to quiet her troubled mind. Sitting next to her, and snuggling as close as possible with body language that meant comfort, I started reading aloud to her. To my amazement, the sobbing subsided, and often she would drop off to sleep. The subject matter of the reading material was not what brought comfort and solace. Rather, it was my body language and the reading aloud. From then on I kept my Bible or an inspirational book near the couch. The content may have made little or no difference to her, but each time I was enriched by the reading.

After her death, our oldest son, a journalist, paid tribute to his mother at her memorial service by thanking her for giving him a love of reading. As he made this statement, I remembered that one of Wilma's great joys was to read aloud to the children before they could read for themselves. Sitting in a chair, or later on the couch, with one, two, three, or even all four children, both mother and children would be transported to another world as the story unfolded. Somewhere in the dimness of what remained to her, the reading aloud, sitting on the couch, and the resulting joy, must have brought tranquility to her troubled spirit.

Our Struggles with Bathing

Caregivers often encounter great difficulty with bathing the person with Alzheimer's. Various theories have been proposed, but no one is really sure what is going on in the mind of the person with Alzheimer's. One woman wrote, "I never thought that I would have to fight with my mother like I fought with my children over taking a bath." Soaking in a tub of hot water or singing in the shower carries images of relaxation and special pleasure. That is not always true for the person with Alzheimer's.

For us the change began to take place when Wilma would not get into the tub when the water was already run. Different healthcare persons, who by this time were assisting us under the auspices of Hospice Palliative Care, tried various ways, but every one failed. I tried with the shower, but when the water hit her, she escaped from the shower. It was time for imagination. I installed a new showerhead with a flexible hose, thinking that I could control the stream of water so that it would not hit her face. My first attempt was a disaster. As soon as the water was directed at her she escaped again, sending water all over the floor, and I was soaking wet.

I gave up for the time being and gave her sponge baths, because what should have been a relaxing, calming time in the bathtub became a time of screaming. I had to explain the difficulty to some of my neighbors; I didn't want them to think I was a wife beater.

Wilma had always had a fear of water, which kept her from enjoying swimming. She was never able to conquer that fear, especially when her nose and eyes were under water. When Alzheimer's was added to this deep-seated fear of water, tub bathing was impossible and showers were frightening, resulting in wild resistance.

However, resolution was near. Since I was already getting wet, I removed my clothes and got into the tub with her. There was no conflict. I could turn on the shower, making sure the water was warm and gentle. She didn't resist, and we both got clean. That system worked for us until she died. It was a radical shift for me, but it was a solution that I know no health-care worker in an institution could have provided for her. And, after more than fifty years of marriage, we had discovered the joy of taking a shower together.

In Love All Over Again

Adjustments were made when Wilma started walking at night. We went out together, regardless of the hour, and walked. When steps became a problem, I learned to find walking routes that didn't involve steps. Meals were a problem, restaurants were difficult, so I became a cook.

With each step in Wilma's decline came the need for flexibility and new changes. Sometimes her changes were subtle, sometimes dramatic. I always had to be on constant alert and to continually develop a new plan of action. With each change came the need for me to change as well.

Yet this was a time when wonderful new bonding took place.

The changes occurring for Wilma were devastating. Yet I realized that what was emerging in me was good. Wilma was not the same person I had fallen in love with more than fifty years before. However, the long hours of continued contact through feeding, walking, reading, bathing, and dressing had nurtured an entirely new love with a new person. Surprisingly, at age seventy-five, I was in love all over again.

FOR FURTHER THOUGHT...

Creative imagination is required to meet the challenges brought on by Alzheimer's. Changes brought on by the disease may be very subtle, or they may be traumatic. But they are inexorable. The caregiver must be flexible. What works one day may not work the next. I was finding that the solutions were limited only by my imagination.

Even though it seemed we were on a whitewater raft with new currents and uncertainties always coming upon us, still, in the midst of Wilma's confusion and my struggles to cope, there came tranquility beyond belief. I can explain that peace best with a scriptural reference. It is "the peace of God that surpasses all understanding" (Philippians 4:7). It is the peace of God, and our minds cannot contrive it or produce it. It is a gift to be received by placing ourselves and those whom we hold dear, and all of life, in the hands of God who will direct us through the rough waters ahead.

Chapter 5

HELPFUL HINTS FOR THE JOURNEY

The person with Alzheimer's is locked into a condition that makes change almost impossible. Therefore, the caregiving and the caregiver must change. From my reading and my day-to-day experience, I was able to find helpful hints for my caregiving.

In the past, reality orientation was thought to help the person back to reality, i.e., "No, I'm not your Uncle John, I'm your son." The theory was that it would help the patient connect with the real world. However, I found that repeatedly correcting Wilma and attempting to make some contact with reality either brought hostility or withdrawal. In every case the result was negative.

The caregiver can validate, or at least accept, the patient's version of reality. If the Alzheimer's patient asks about her long-dead mother, there is no point in stating, "You know your mother died ten years ago." It is better to say something like, "You really miss her, don't you?" Likely or not the patient does not remember her mother's death, and for that moment, her mother is alive to her.

Diversionary therapy works too. The goal here is to foster conversation by gently changing the subject. Instead of talking about her dead mother, move the conversation to one or more wonderful qualities of her mother. Engage the patient as much as she wishes to be engaged around the happy connection that she can make with her mother.

Building a Support Team

To have strength for this journey, build a personal Alzheimer's support team. The family doctor, a clinical psychologist who specializes in Alzheimer's, and an Alzheimer's support group provide the needed help. (More details about the support team will be found in Chapter Six, about resources for the journey.) Because each person with Alzheimer's has his or her own special needs, it is likely that someone in a support group has had some experiences with particular situations similar to those the caregiver is facing. We need that help from the support group, because collectively those people will have more daily experiences with the disease than many professionals may have.

A person climbing a mountain is told to not look up to the top of the mountain, but rather to look down at his feet and be sure of the next step. One can find strength for the next step, and in due time the mountaintop will be reached. The Alzheimer's caregiver does the same thing. We take one step at a time, using the strength and resources available at that moment.

I urge caregivers to draw upon their understanding of God, even a limited understanding. I could not then and cannot now answer any of the "why" questions about Alzheimer's. Peace came for me when I could walk away from the "why" questions and not devote any more of my energy to those thoughts. Of course that "why" still remains unanswered. My best answer came to me one night in the middle of deep despair. It seemed as though God was saying to me, "I am still here." The awareness of God's presence was enough. It was then, and continues to be now, all I needed.

The Wind at My Back

Help for the journey came for me in surprising ways. I came to the point of saying, "I live on the edge of surprise." These surprises came in unexpected and small ways. When I focused on caring for Wilma as my only agenda, I discovered an unbelievable power released in me. For one thing, with her as my only responsibility, I did not have to plan or even think about other things to do. I was no longer at war with myself but could devote all of my energies to this one task. Instead of facing the wind, I now had the wind at my back.

During a period when Wilma was highly agitated, I was deeply concerned and bewildered. Sleep had become more difficult, and my days and nights seemed to flow together. One morning, about 3 A.M., when I could not sleep, I sensed God saying to me, "You take care of Wilma, and I'll take care of you." In the darkness of that night there was **brightness**. In the loneliness of my journey there was **presence**. In my despair, there was **hope**. I fell asleep. For the next five years that one moment carried me through the tests that were yet to come. I had experienced what some Christian mystics refer to as an epiphany. It was then, and is now, a holy moment for me, and one I will always cherish.

It carried me through many difficult days that followed. I came to trust through every valley and through all the darkness that followed. The 23rd Psalm became a new reality for me.

Adversity seems to make a person more sensitive. Often it is during these times that insight will come, something beyond the normal thought process. In adversity comes discovery. When Columbus discovered the new world, he did not create the new world. His searching brought him to what was already there. When a prospector discovers gold, he finds what was already there. When a researcher discovers a new method, he finds what already exists.

The adversity we encountered with Alzheimer's not only made me more sensitive but also sent me on a path to an interesting discovery. The weeks, months, and years of caring for Wilma gave me much more time to reflect and gather ideas that would have escaped me in the usual crush of daily activities. One of the ideas that emerged during these days was the value of what I call "setting our wills."

I commented before that in our wedding vows we were asked, "Will you...love...till death parts?" The question put to us was not "Are you able?" or "Do you know enough?" or "Are you capable?" But rather it was "Will you?"

When I embarked on this journey with Alzheimer's and affirmed, "I will do all in my power to delay and hopefully avoid institutional care for Wilma," I discovered a strength to go on which was beyond my power to comprehend.

All the Help We Can Get

In the early stages of Alzheimer's, the pain of the diagnosis is so personal and so intense that we must have all the support from others that we can get. In earlier days, Alzheimer's was thought of as mental illness or even related to some earlier deviant lifestyle. It carried with it an element of shame. Now we know that Alzheimer's is a brain disease; it will get worse over time, and it is not curable but treatable. The disease is not normal aging forgetfulness, it is not simply an emotional problem, and it is not contagious. It is important to accept the fact of Alzheimer's as early as possible. Then the help and support needed can come earlier rather than later.

In the earlier days, I felt that I was all alone. I would not talk with Wilma about Alzheimer's. I did not talk with family and friends. That changed as I took hold of the reality of the disease and eventually sought help for the journey.

Gradually, as Wilma's illness progressed, her dependence on me increased and the care she required became more demanding. Receiving help from someone else was a spur-of-the moment response, but it became an integral part of the caregiving I needed for Wilma.

People would ask me, "If I can be of help sometime, give me a call." I would reply with a polite "thank you," but I did not follow through. One day, when I received an offer of help, I didn't accept—at least I didn't at first. But I asked for the person's phone number, and later that same day, I forced myself to call that person to ask if the offer was still being made. This gave the person a chance to decline, but it didn't happen—not then, not ever.

We established the day and time for the first visit. I said it should not exceed one hour. The first volunteer and I discussed on the phone any questions she had and suggestions I had. Then when she came, I introduced her to Wilma and left. This abrupt introduction avoided any refusal or negative action on Wilma's part and left the two of them to negotiate what would happen next.

On this first "in-home respite visit," I determined to be home in forty-five minutes or less to avoid panic if some difficulty developed. This gave the three of us time to relax, discuss how the time went, and arrange for a next visit. So I was beginning to receive assistance. It also meant that regular visitors established some relationship with Wilma, even if she did not remember the person from one visit to the next.

My schedule was always flexible, adjustable to the volunteer's schedule, and in time the respite periods sometimes went for three or four hours. Gradually I became more comfortable with asking for help, and often the respite giver would even recruit another volunteer. So over a period of time, there was a "company of angels."

Each person brought his or her own ability or gift. The volunteers were free to use their own imaginations and creativity to develop on-the-spot activity. In the early days, some of the volunteers encouraged Wilma to do manual things. But during the later stages she did not initiate anything, so everything was done for her.

When Wilma was ambulatory, volunteers took her for long walks away from the house. When she was in a wheelchair, the long rides seemed to be even more enjoyable. For her it was the sense of doing something and going somewhere. The long walks or rides gave opportunity to see various birds, animals, or flowers. Maybe it was the sunset or the sound of lapping water. The sights, smells, sounds, and actions provided an outstanding tapestry that surrounded her day. These respite caregivers enriched her life by putting her in touch with the world around her, even though her ability to process what she saw and heard decreased with each passing day.

Our Visiting "Angels"

These visiting "angels" enabled me to remain alive physically, socially, mentally, and emotionally so that I could care for Wilma. Here is a sampling of a few of the eighty-seven volunteers who provided respite care during the last five years of Wilma's life.

One volunteer brought projects she thought Wilma might enjoy, such as colored art paper. Using scissors, Wilma cut out shapes, any shape, and pasted the shapes on sheets of art paper. It was a simple art form, but an art form done by Wilma and the volunteer. When I returned home, there was genuine joy on her face when it came to "show and tell." Some traces of her former teaching days were being experienced.

For nearly three years another "angel" had ice cream parties at the café in our retirement village. The party was always at the same place with the same people. Everyone knew that chocolate ice cream was Wilma's preference. When her world was falling apart, what better thing could happen than to be the center of attention at an ice-cream party, if only for a brief time?

One couple brought their love for singing and their old songbooks. In the early days, Wilma would join in the singing of the oldies, both hymns and secular songs. With the passing of time, she lost the ability to form words. But if we watched and listened carefully, we could hear her humming the tune or see her foot tapping and catch a smile of acknowledgement. Because Wilma had been a piano teacher and a life-long lover of music, these angels put her in touch with a world deep inside.

Glenn Miller, Sammy Kaye, and other bandleaders of an earlier period offered music that Wilma enjoyed. As the disease broadened and deepened its devastation, this music brought responses when almost nothing else touched her. One afternoon, two respite caregivers came as I was playing a Glenn Miller record. The man had suffered a stroke that limited his speech but not his motor skills. As he came through the door and heard the music, he led with a dancing movement and Wilma followed. The joy on her face as they danced together to the music of Glenn Miller was a pleasure to watch.

Some of the visiting angels prepared small snacks and something to drink. When Wilma's speech was almost gone, or she refused to enter in, the angel went ahead with the preparations anyway. I assured volunteers that even a failure was a success, because Wilma was engaged, and I had time away.

One afternoon a volunteer brought children to our house for a party. There was a wonderful glow on Wilma's face when I returned home that day.

Even though by then nearly all memory was gone, along with most of her ability to speak, it was obvious that Wilma was filled with a deep happiness as she partied with the children.

The elaborate effort to care for my wife, while at the same time electing to live in a full-care retirement community, may raise some questions. My answer to this is that the retirement community was an important component of our life-care plan. It provided emergency nursing home care for Wilma when necessary and occasional day respite care when needed. In addition it gave our children and me the satisfaction of knowing that she would be safe and cared for in the event I preceded her in death.

Over and beyond institutionalizing, which I saw as limiting, was the possibility of living with Alzheimer's without boundaries. I have already noted some of the ways we went beyond the boundaries by using the gifts and talents of numerous volunteers.

Traveling With Wilma

Retirement had brought with it dreams of travel and now, although our travel was much more limited, it was not necessary to stop entirely if I became a bit creative. Traveling with Wilma was a challenge, but I discovered through contact with motel, restaurant, and airline personnel that people would help us.

Our trips by car, from Florida to Ohio and back, required detailed planning and considerable imagination. Choices of daily outfits were mine to make. I needed to pack for both of us. When the car was loaded, the adventure began.

Since Wilma could not handle the details of a bathroom stop without assistance, the usual rest stops along the road were totally confusing to her. But I discovered that motel personnel were quite helpful. When it was time for a rest stop, I would stop at a motel and tell the desk clerk our situation. A clerk would check to see that the ladies room was clear and then wait outside to keep others from coming in until we were finished. We were never refused in this request.

Chain hotels and motels have similar layouts, so we chose a chain that was well dispersed along our Florida to Ohio route. It was my hope that the similarity would be less confusing for Wilma. The typical travel day began with breakfast. I would bring the continental breakfast to our room. After eating, we were ready for travel. When it was time for our first rest stop, I would go to the same motel chain, if possible, estimate where we would be when it was time to stop for the night, and ask the clerk to reserve a room for us at the motel up ahead. I also found that the motel would be willing to give us the fruit and rolls left over from the breakfast. That would become our lunch.

When we arrived at our evening destination, I would find the nearest good restaurant and order meals to take out. Often when I explained our situation, the clerk would bring our dinner to the car when ready so that I could stay in the car with Wilma. When we checked into our motel, I took Wilma in with me during the registration process. I needed to have continuous contact with her. Travel carries enough uncertainties; a wandering wife was the last thing I needed.

After check-in, we proceeded to our room and were ready for our evening meal. Fortunately, we never had any serious problems. I tried to keep familiar patterns with eating, sleeping, and bathroom functions. If I was able to keep the frustration level low, Wilma often slept while I was driving—although I knew that if she slept too much it might be more difficult to get her to sleep at night.

By this time, I had learned to sleep with a light on in the bedroom. When she would awaken at night, there was always confusion and disorientation. Over time I made the adjustment and was able to leave a light on all night, every night. This became a requirement, even when we were at home.

After Wilma was asleep, I would prepare for the next day of travel. I would lay out our clothes for the next day and put away that day's travel clothes. I checked the map and our motel book to see where we would be about lunchtime and where we could stop the next night. In this way we were able to make the trip to and from Ohio and Florida.

Travel by air presented other challenges, but travel personnel helped us. I always requested a wheel chair, which meant we were given special attention and priority. This was before the terrorist attacks of 9/11, so security was not as tight. Still, we always got to the airport early so as to be at the right gate, with at least one hour to spare. I would push the wheel chair around while we waited, which gave me extra exercise. For added safety, I had a bracelet for Wilma to wear that had our home phone number on it.

Our biggest trip was to visit three of our children, two in California and one in North Dakota. We wanted about three to four days in each location. The entire trip went without incident. On one of the longer legs of the journey, about an hour before landing, a cabin attendant came to our seats. She told me she was a nurse and wondered if there was anything she could do for us. I explained our situation and asked if she thought she could assist Wilma to the bathroom. So she took Wilma by the hand and led her down the aisle to the back of the plane. They disappeared inside the little lavatory, which is rather small for two people. But soon they were back and the attendant said, "Mission accomplished."

FOR FURTHER THOUGHT…

Be aware of the changes in the person you are caring for. You, as the caregiver, are the one who must adapt, be flexible, and help the patient through the changes in his or her own life.

The years with an Alzheimer's patient can be long and torturous. It seemed that we had been through nearly every aberration of the disease: paranoia, pacing (sometimes for hours at a time, day or night), violent outbursts, and later almost total silence. I was surviving, but sometimes I wondered how long.

Once a friend came to provide respite and a rare opportunity for me to attend Sunday morning worship. During the service we were singing the words by George Croly, "Spirit of God, Descend upon My Heart." We came to the second stanza: "I ask no dream, no prophet ecstasies, no sudden rending of the veil of clay. No angel visitant, no opening skies, But take the dimness of my soul away." My fragile emotions shattered. I could not sing but muttered the words while tears flowed down my cheeks. The congregation finished the song, and the dimness of my soul lifted. Once more a verse of Scripture, from John 14:18, became a living word to me: "I will not leave you."

Be willing to reach out for help. For five years volunteers helped me with Wilma. They were kind, creative, and brought new interest and diversion into her life. They helped me to get away for my own personal renewal. And I needed it to continue to give myself to Wilma's care.

Figure out how others can step in to help. Think about what you need and when you need it. Then enlist help. Soon you will have your own band of "angels" to help you on this journey.

Chapter 6

* *

RESOURCES FOR THE JOURNEY

Various resources were helpful to me during our journey with Alzheimer's. We had a good medical team. Our physician, a neurologist, and a clinical psychologist each made a significant contribution, especially as they worked together as a team. Since we were living in two places, we established such a team both in Ohio and in Florida. The local Alzheimer's Association can point caregivers to helpful medical people. Once a good team is formed, I found that it is best to trust them. For the most part, it may be unwise to continually seek alternative medical help.

An important part of the care program is an Alzheimer's support group. The Alvin A. Dubin Alzheimer's Resource Center of Fort Myers, Florida, was most helpful and put me in touch with a nearby Alzheimer's support group. I've discovered that similar resource centers can be found in most communities. Not only does a support group help with day-by-day experience that they can offer the caregiver, but also it gives the caregiver a social outlet during what can become a very isolated time. I found that group support was important for my emotional health.

Also, the Alzheimer's group made me aware of other groups or organizations that provide assistance, such as in-home assistance or adult day care or meals on wheels. I found that there is a lot of assistance available in the community.

Many churches have the Stephen Ministry as part of their program. The Stephen Ministry offers a group of specially trained lay people who provide many forms of assistance to people in need. It is worthwhile to contact churches to see if they have a Stephen Ministry and then to connect with the Stephen Ministry leader to see if there is a way or ways that they can help you.

We regularly attended Sunday morning worship services until my wife became disruptive. The worship experience was an additional source of strength for me. The local congregation was an added resource for fellowship and support. It also provided a large number of people (the angels) who readily responded to requests for help. I was to learn that people did need to be asked. Few will encroach on the caregiver without an invitation.

I also found that I needed to meet with an attorney to work over all the legal documents, taking into account our particular situation. There is no general document or documents that will cover all of the special needs when Alzheimer's is involved, so the directives of a good attorney are important. Planning for end-of-life concerns is, I believe, most important.

The early diagnosis of Alzheimer's gave us the opportunity to resolve many concerns while Wilma was still quite aware and still able to talk. We discussed every aspect of our final days and put every thing in writing, sending a copy to each of our children. This would provide for Wilma in the event that I should die first. Once we had moved through this entire discussion and resolved every eventuality to the best of our ability, we never discussed it again. We then proceeded to do all we could to make each remaining day the best day possible.

Another important resource for our journey with Alzheimer's was the services of Hospice. I must admit that Hospice was not on my "radar-planning screen" until our family physician asked our permission to refer us to Hospice. The referral is necessary for Hospice to initiate their services. Looking back, I can see how our lives were wonderfully enhanced by Hospice, and it is difficult to imagine how we could have endured without the assistance of this wonderful organization.

Following our physician's referral, Hospice responded by sending a team to our home for their evaluation and to determine if and when they could begin their assistance. Since there is a linkage between Medicare and Hospice, the guidelines for services are established by Medicare. When it was determined that we qualified, we learned the services would begin immediately, for an initial period of ninety days, and this could be renewed for an additional ninety days.

Services outlined were for a one-hour-per-week visit from a health-aide person who could assist in bathing, feeding, or general care, as needed. During the contract days, Medicare would pay for all medical supplies, including prescriptions. In addition, a Hospice chaplain was assigned to us, and the social worker made regular visits.

For us, our journey with Alzheimer's had long stretches of time when Wilma's situation would plateau; then there would be a rapid decline in weight or ability. We learned that Hospice was readily available for as long as our situation met the guidelines. The end result was that Hospice was available to us as needed during the last four years of our journey. Because we spent the summer months in Ohio and the winter months in Florida, we discovered that the services of Hospice were available anywhere, so long as the guidelines were met.

In addition to the help we received from individuals and groups, I did a lot of reading on the subject of Alzheimer's. Our local Alzheimer's office had a large number of books about the disease and advice for the caregiver. And I found the Bible to be a great source of strength to me. I had used the Bible in my sermon preparation for fifty years and had studied Greek for three years at the theological seminary, but now it was personal, and its truths were a blessing and a source of strength to me. They became so clear to me at the point of my despair. I found rich nuggets of gold in the Psalms and the New Testament and would suggest to others dealing with an Alzheimer's patient to read either a traditional or more modern translation.

The Value of Stories

Another important help for me was other people's stories. I remember a man who had an appliance business and was an avid golfer. When Alzheimer's was taking over his life, his sales and office staff ran the business for him, even though his own attention to business details was severely impaired.

But it was his golf game that brought the greatest distress to his friends. They had played together for years, but now one friend was assigned to him for each game. The assigned friend monitored every stroke he made to watch where the ball landed, because he could no longer remember where his ball was and could never find it. Then it became too much of a chore, and after a particularly difficult game, the foursome broke up.

I know what this kind of breakup means. Those kinds of endings have to be recognized and allowed to come. That story of the golfer helped me when

Wilma and I had to give up playing table games. We had tried bridge several times, but never got the hang of it. But we enjoyed several table games. Nevertheless, the time came when Wilma could no longer manage the sequence concept. For a year or two we played with friends who did not mind that after I played my turn, I would assist Wilma with hers. But then that became too difficult, and we had to end our games with friends.

We tried playing table games at home, just the two of us. I would manage her game and mine and did it so that very often she would win. But then the games became totally confusing for her, so we stopped playing.

I learned much from others who helped me when something ended or a new thing needed to be incorporated into our lives. People who were caregivers were also my teachers.

I discovered that it is vitally important for a caregiver to develop some diversion that takes a person completely away from the normal activities of the day, some activity that brings maximum pleasure. I improved on my woodworking, making several pieces of furniture for the house. When I found someone who would stay with my wife, I was able to enjoy some fishing. An acquaintance of mine, whose wife had Parkinson's disease, took up the hobby of counted cross-stitch. He spent more and more time with his new hobby as his wife's health declined, especially after he was required to be at home twenty-four hours a day. Later, his counted cross-stitch was judged best of show at the Florida State Fair.

The Symphony of the Morning

Exercise is so important for the caregiver's well-being. I enjoyed walking, even in the rain. It was invigorating. I became more aware of the sights and sounds around me. One morning I was walking in a heavy fog along Lake Erie and heard a freighter sound its foghorn. With the song of birds, the colors and shapes of rocks and trees and flowers, I wrote in my journal that "I have heard the symphony of the morning, and it was a free concert." I found there were so many resources and helps available to me at little or no cost.

Psalm 8:4 says, "What are human beings that you are mindful of them?" We live in a universe of countless wonders: craggy mountains, lush green meadows, deep forests, great blue lakes, delightful bubbling streams. Each one of us can add many other descriptive words and phrases. How is it that in the midst of all this the Creator has time for me? I was made aware in a marvelous, unmistakable way that God knew all about my troubles and was not going to leave me alone, no matter what.

Recap of resources for the journey:

1. The medical team.
2. The local Alzheimer's resource center or go to www.alzfdn.org or www.alz.org. Some

Alzheimer's centers provide a card which reads, "Please direct your conversation to me. My companion has Alzheimer's."
3. The local Hospice unit.
4. Your own God-given IMAGINATION.
5. Some books that I found helpful:
    1. Wayne Ewing, *Tears in God's Bottle*. Tucson, AZ: White Stone Circle Press, 1999.
    2. Nancy Sparks, *The Notebook*. New York: Warner Books, Inc., 1996.
    3. Nancy L. Mace and Peter V. Robins. *The 36-Hour Day*. New York: Warner Books, Inc., 1992.
    4. Mitch Albom, *Tuesdays With Morrie*. New York: Bantam Doubleday Dell Publishing Group, Inc., 1997.
    5. Terry A. Anderson, *Den of Lion*. New York: Ballantine Books, 1993.
    6. Howard Rutledge, *In the Presence of Mine Enemies*. Old Tappan, NJ: Fleming H. Revell, 1993.
    7. Harold S. Kushner, *The Lord is My Shepherd*. New York: Alfred A. Knoph, 2003.
    8. Robert Davis, *My Journey into Alzheimer's Disease*. Wheaton, IL: Tyndale House Publishers, Inc., 1989.
    9. Bill Beckwith, *Managing Your Memory*. Boulder, CO: Bookworks, 2004.

10. Lisa P. Gwyther, *You Are One of Us*. Durham, NC: Duke University Medical Center, 1995.
11. William M. Grubbs, *In Sickness and in Health*. Forest Knolls, CA: Eden Books, 1997.
12. Robertson McQuilkin, *Living by Vows*. Columbia, SC: Columbia International University, 1990.
13. Carol Simpson, *At the Heart of Alzheimer's*. Gaithersburg, MD: Manor Healthcare Corp., 1996.

FOR FURTHER THOUGHT...

In *The Notebook,* Nancy Sparks writes, "Alzheimer's is a barren disease, as empty and lifeless as a desert." For the victim, this is quite possibly true. However, life abounds—even in the desert. To the unfamiliar and untrained eye, the desert is foreboding terrain. But to those who traverse it daily, subtle signs of life, even to a sublime sense of beauty, can be found.

What about the caregiver? Is all lost? Is the caregiver confined only to breathe winds of despair that blow through the caregiver's heart and soul as surely as the hot currents that constantly shift the shape of dry sand?

I found an answer to this question that is best described by Wayne Ewing in *Tears in God's Bottle,* when he reflected on Luke 11:20, "But if it is by the finger of God that I cast out demons, then the kingdom of God has come to you." He writes, "Ultimately, I realized that in the face of Alzheimer's disease, care is the finger of God. The mere extension of kindness—a smile, a hug, a kiss, a brushing my loved one's hair, feeding her, dressing her, applying makeup to her, or singing a song, invited God to reach into an evil I myself could not penetrate. As a result, I now know that evil cringes in the presence of such focused, attentive love. Affection, although incapable of curing the disease, heals the wounds of the person assaulted, for affection is the finger of God."

After years of struggle with this hideous evil, I was able to learn that the desert was not completely void of life and that the darkness of the tunnel was not total. I learned that there can be peace in the storm, joy in the midst of heartache, freedom in captivity, and hope out of despair.

I did not choose the journey with Alzheimer's. Who would? But, I am deeply grateful for what I learned along the way. This book would not have been written, these insights would not have been gained, were it not for the tragedy. My profound appreciation and thanks to Wilma.

Chapter 7

. . . .

ALZHEIMER'S UP CLOSE

During the fourth year of our journey with Alzheimer's we moved to Shell Point, a life-care retirement community in Fort Myers, Florida. We also kept our home in Ohio. At Shell Point there were lighted walkways around the more than one-mile perimeter that allowed us to walk in safety, day or night. I also enjoyed working in a small garden that we had at Shell Point.

Our choice of Shell Point life-care retirement community brought several factors into focus. First, was the option of warmer winter weather. Second, was the security Shell Point offered, given the unknown in the journey ahead. Third, our children were released from the responsibility of placement in some institution when that might be necessary. Fourth, we were assured by contract that together or separately we would be cared for the rest of our lives. My resolve to "do all in my power to delay and hopefully avoid total institutional care" took shape during the next several years.

What follows is a look at a typical period of time during this fourth year (since diagnosis) of Alzheimer's. The caregiver faces days like these and needs to know that this is the way life will be with an Alzheimer's patient.

Thursday 4:00 A.M. Wilma awoke with considerable shaking. She was not as hot and sweaty as at other times but was disoriented, with moderate speech difficulty. I gave her an anxiety pill, and we both went back to sleep.

7:00 A.M. We awoke, and Wilma was shaky but quite clear. She talked about her fears. She was now afraid of our children coming for a visit.

8:45 A.M. She had her regular medication, and after breakfast we went for a short walk and stopped to talk with a neighbor. I referred to the fact that we had once planned to travel but now that was impossible because of our situation. This was very disturbing to Wilma, because she rightly understood that we did not travel because of her condition. I knew then that I had to be more careful about this kind of conversation.

1:00 P.M. She took her regular medication, and then we ate lunch. We had a hair appointment for 3:15 P.M., but Wilma simply could not face the idea, so we cancelled. This brought on so much anxiety that we walked the entire perimeter of the Island of

Shell Point and added a walk around the interior circle before returning home. Now she was worn out, so she slept briefly until I prepared a pizza. But Wilma did not eat much. She wasn't hungry but did take her medication. She lay down on the couch and slept until about 8:00 P.M. when she awakened, and I gave her the prescribed sleeping pill. She slept through the night with the exception of two trips to the bathroom, and appeared to be clear and not anxious when she awoke the next morning.

Friday 6:00 A.M. Wilma ate her oatmeal and had generally fair speech.

8:30 A.M. We walked, and Wilma recognized other people and seemed happy to talk with friends. When we returned home at 9:00 A.M., she immediately fell asleep.

9:30 A.M. She awoke startled and was not sure who our daughter, Marilyn, was. She was able to recount a dream about a palm tree blowing down in high winds.

7:30 P.M. She took her sleeping pill and her regular medication and went to sleep.

Saturday 2:00 A.M. Wilma awoke somewhat confused but not panicky. By 7:00 A.M. we were out walking. When we got back home, she did not sleep, but we were gradually able to get ready for lunch with friends.

11:30 A.M. We were able to have lunch with friends. Afterward I tried to get her to nap but couldn't, and by 4:00 P.M. we were visited by friends. She needed another anxiety pill.

7:30 P.M. I tried to read to her in bed, but she was up and down several times until about 9:00 P.M., so I gave her an anxiety pill. Soon she was asleep.

Sunday 2:30 A.M. Wilma needed more medication, but by 5:30 A.M. she was wide-awake, so we walked around the court. When we returned she said, "Now my stomach is full." I think she was referring to a nervous feeling in her stomach. I noticed sometimes that she would hold her stomach when the anxiety reached a panic level. I gave her the anxiety medication. By 7:00 A.M. she was asleep, and it appeared to be a relaxed sleep.

11:15 A.M. We went to the grocery store for supplies. She broke out in a sweat and was very confused and agitated, speaking with disconnected phrases that meant nothing. These public outbursts in a grocery store could be embarrassing but not disruptive. When we had tried attending a church worship service, her outbursts were disruptive, and so we stopped attending, except on rare occasions when I could attend while a volunteer stayed with Wilma.

6:30 P.M. She had her medication with dinner but ate only a little of her meal. Took another walk around the court and then turned on television. But she soon asked me to turn it off.

8:15 P.M. Wilma took a sleeping pill and slept soundly until 1:45 A.M., when she awoke totally disoriented, asking questions that made no sense. She went to the bathroom and started shaking, so I gave her an anxiety pill.

1:45 A.M. Since she could not sleep, she put on her robe and we walked around the court and she seemed clearer, more rational, and relatively calm.

2:15 A.M. We returned to the apartment and she went to sleep immediately.

Monday 5:15 A.M. Wilma awakened somewhat confused but went back to sleep until 6:00 A.M. When she came into the kitchen where I was laying out materials for a woodworking project, I told her that a friend was coming to stay with her. She fell apart. "I can't do it," she said. We went for a walk, and she began to work with the idea that a friend was coming.

7:15 A.M. After our walk, she went to sleep on the couch and awoke about 8:30, still very much concerned that a friend was coming. But after much conversation she said, "I'll try."

10:00 A.M. Wilma had taken an anxiety pill before the friend arrived. She expressed great happiness at her friend's coming. The three of us walked to the woodshop. Then the two women went another direction, and I went to the shop. We were apart for two hours.

12:15 P.M. We took our friend to the Shell Point dining room for lunch, but Wilma could eat only a little soup, melon, and ice cream. We finally left and went back to the apartment, where Wilma warmly expressed her gratefulness to her friend.

2:00 P.M. Wilma took an anxiety pill and was soon asleep, probably more from exhaustion than from the pill. But she awakened at 3:45 P.M. agitated, disoriented, and shaking. By 7:30 P.M., she was in bed, and with the help of a sleeping pill, slept through the night, except briefly for a trip to the bathroom at 2:45 A.M.

Tuesday 6:00 A.M. Wilma awakened and her speech was comparatively good. She formed words and was in touch. She slept for another 30 minutes on the couch.

8:30 A.M. We ate breakfast and went for a long walk.

4:00 P.M. Wilma had an appointment with the psychologist. That night she slept briefly but was awakened at 11:00 P.M. by a dream about her mother. She couldn't identify anything more except she awoke saying, "Mother, Mother." So we went for a walk, and when we returned home, she went right to sleep.

Wednesday 4:00 A.M. Yesterday had been a good day, and I thought that perhaps we had turned a corner. But with this disease we never turn a corner, we just have an occasional variance in behavior.

She wanted to talk about her mother and father and about dying. "When will it occur?" she asked. "Why does it take so long?"

4:40 A.M. I prepared tea and toast for the two of us. It was a difficult day. She was very distressed about remembering my name, repeating it over and over hundreds of times. I had tried on other similar occasions to stop her from this kind of endless repetition, but that only proved to be more frustrating. After breakfast, which took several attempts to eat, we took two walks. When we got home, she took an anxiety pill and fell asleep.

9:00 A.M. For much of the day, she was trying to figure out why I was outside of her family. She had three brothers and two sisters. There was just enough understanding to realize that I was not part of that family. We talked about parents and how babies are started but could not find a way to bridge the gap. Finally she said, "I'm tired; tell me about my mother." I told her about funny things that happened in her family, and she started laughing. Then we were able to go on to other things.

1:00 P.M. We left in the car to take friends to the airport. At 3:00 P.M., when we returned, we went for a walk. Afterwards she went to sleep for a half-hour.

6:00 P.M. A neighbor brought us a beautiful dinner. Wilma picked at it a bit.

9:00 P.M. She took a sleeping pill but was up three different times and came into the room where I was reading. At 10:45 P.M., I went to bed with her.

Thursday 6:00 A.M. Wilma awakened shaking and a bit sweaty. I gave her an anxiety pill, and she spent the next hour talking about people who were telling her to eat more. "If I don't eat, I'll die," she said. It seemed that every day there was some discussion about dying. Sometimes it frightened her, sometimes it was just matter of fact. She went back to sleep at 7:00 A.M. We walked that day, and the day was uneventful. By 9:00 P.M. she was in bed and asleep.

Friday we had hoped to drive over to visit friends but had to call and cancel. They came to our place instead, but Wilma was so disoriented that she refused to join us as we ate ice cream.

Saturday 3:00 A.M. Wilma awoke confused. She was startled by a dream. There is difficulty in discerning the difference between a dream and reality. Incoherent talking continued, and at one point she asked, "What am I doing wrong, and how can I stop it?"

6:30 A.M. She was forming words correctly, yet her sentences were incoherent and erratic. By 7:00 A.M., she was able to lie down on the couch and nap. Later, we were able to go to the grocery store, and she was only a little anxious. All in all, it was a good morning.

5:00 P.M. Wilma was not eating much of anything. She had oatmeal for breakfast but needed to return to the bowl several times before completing it. She would not eat lunch, so I gave her a fortified health drink. We took a walk to our garden, where I picked some beans. When we returned home, she slept briefly while I prepared dinner. She woke up very anxious so we took another walk. When we got back, she was not hungry. So I gave her another fortified health drink. So she ate very little that day.

9:00 P.M. Wilma had gone to bed but then got up and wanted to talk. Then she asked me to lie down with her. I read one hymn, and she was fast asleep, happily, for the whole night.

Sunday 6:30 A.M. She awoke and was forming words perfectly. We took a long walk and then had breakfast, but Wilma only ate half of a piece of toast. She did not want lunch and did not eat supper except for a couple of spoonfuls of soup. We took another long walk around the entire perimeter of the community.

This was a very difficult day. She talked constantly, but only occasionally was she understandable. She again had difficulty with who I am. "Are you really Floyd?" she would ask. She looked at my picture then at me and said that they were not the same person. She couldn't remember my mother and father. Making any genuine connections was difficult. This continued with much talking until time for sleep.

9:00 P.M. She took her sleeping pill but was still wide-awake ninety minutes later. Since it had been many hours since her last anxiety pill, I gave her another. She remained wakeful, even though I tried many things that had worked before. She finally fell asleep at about 12:30 and slept until 5:00 A.M.

Wilma awoke confused and agitated. The day before I had told her about my plan to go fishing with a friend and who would come and stay with her while I was away. How was her brain processing this today? Was she afraid I would leave her? Did she resent my fishing trip? Was she apprehensive about the person who would be staying with her? I don't know. I cancelled the fishing trip.

Many mornings she would awake startled and confused, but she could not explain it clearly since her words didn't make sense. She was anxious but couldn't explain the source of her anxiety. Sometimes she would return to sleep after I had talked with her.

Sometimes she would ask for a pill, and if enough time had elapsed since the previous one, I would give it to her. But shortly, she might be demanding another pill. Nothing I said would change her thinking. When this happened, I tried to divert her attention to something else or give her one-fourth of an aspirin, hoping this would satisfy her that she had had her pill.

There were times when she would sleep without any medication at all. Other times, nothing I did would help her get to sleep. One day she might wake up very agitated, but the next day tell me, "I feel wonderful."

And so the days went by. I never knew how she would be in the morning or how the day would go.

During the many years of care giving, I learned that people with Alzheimer's may confuse their days and nights, sleeping at times during the day and then being very active at night. My own sleep time was often interrupted by my wife's activity at all hours or any hour of the night. Fortunately, I was blessed with two natural traits that enabled me to survive. One, for all of my adult life I could function very well on four or five hours of sleep. Two, a catnap of ten minutes at almost any time or any place would revive me, and I was ready to go again. So the loss of sleep or interrupted sleep was never a problem for me.

FOR FURTHER THOUGHT...

The Bible says, "Give thanks in all circum-stances" (1 Thessalonians 5:18). When I read this one day, I was near a low point of despair in my struggle with this sickness that was bringing ruin to everything I knew. It nearly stripped me of the last vestiges of my faith. But I recalled having read, *In the Presence of Mine Enemies* by Howard Rutledge. He was a pilot during the Vietnam War, when he was shot down and placed in the prison known as the Hanoi Hilton.

Physical and mental torture was a daily occur-rence for Rutledge. He was slowly starving to death, because he could not swallow the daily portion of cold seaweed and fat pork. He confessed that he had spent little time thinking about God, leaving that responsibility to his wife. He remembered that she always prayed before they ate. Calling upon his limited reserves and his memory, the next time his food was brought to him, he paused to repeat what he remembered of his wife's table grace. For the first time, he was able to swallow the food.

That picture of Howard Rutledge giving thanks for horrible food, while also being tortured and living in solitary confinement, was unforgettable. I said to myself, "If Howard Rutledge was able to give thanks under those circumstances, then I can say thanks in my situation." Indeed I had discovered that it is possible to "give thanks in all circumstances."

Each person will find his or her own pathway, but if one is to move beyond the despair that I was facing, then there must be a way to construct a meaningful life in the face of disaster.

Others have done so; I needed to find out how I was to do it. For me, it came when I decided that I would give thanks in everything. Every morning was to be my time to be thankful for a new day. It is not foolishness to start the day as did the psalmist long ago, recognizing, "This is the day the Lord has made, let us rejoice and be glad in it" (Psalm 118:24).

I did not give thanks for the Alzheimer's, but I chose to give thanks in spite of the Alzheimer's. I looked around me and found a multitude of things for which I could give thanks, and that rescued me from despair.

Chapter 8

. . . .
KEEP YOUR FORK

I don't know who first told this story, but it reso-
nates with me. There was a woman who had
been diagnosed with a terminal illness. She was
given three months to live. As she was getting her
things in order, she contacted her pastor and had him
come to the house to discuss certain aspects of her
final wishes. She told him which songs she wanted
to have sung at her funeral service, what Scriptures
she would like read, and what outfit she wanted to
be buried in.

Everything was in order, and the pastor was
preparing to leave when the woman added another
detail that was important to her. "There's one more
thing," she said. "What's that?" he replied. "I want
to be buried with a fork in my hand."

The pastor stood looking at the woman, not knowing quite what to say. "That surprises you, doesn't it?" said the woman. "Well, to be honest, I am puzzled by the request," he said. The woman explained, "In all my years of attending church suppers, I remember that when the dishes from the main course were being cleared, someone would inevitably say, 'Keep your fork.' It was my favorite part, because I knew something better was coming, like velvety chocolate cake or deep-dish apple pie. Something wonderful was ahead. So I just want people to see me there in the casket with a fork in my hand and to realize that the best is yet to come."

I remember the news stories about Flight 800 out of New York, bound for Europe. Shortly after takeoff, the plane exploded and everyone died. When we were told that Wilma had Alzheimer's, it was as if we were waiting to board the airplane, but we hadn't taken off yet. But death was certain. It was the only release from this disease. We just did not know what would occur between diagnosis and the end.

The Value of Early Diagnosis

We had no clue about what was going to transpire during the next nine years. As I look back over those years, I am convinced that the early diagnosis was best for us. We could better understand the various suggested treatments and be more open with the doctors about what we were experiencing. As time goes by, I believe more strongly in early diagnosis, because new medications are constantly coming on the market. These are treatments that may delay the onslaught of Alzheimer's and may improve the quality of life.

Moving from denial to acceptance was a difficult but necessary task. Looking back, I realize I should have sought more help, especially from the volunteer community. When I did talk with others about the illness, I did not lose one friend, but I did gain many new friends along the way.

Our Options for Health Care

While I am more impulsive, Wilma needed time to process the data. With the diagnosis, there came time for research, discussion, and decisions. Our options for health care were in-home care, which would at the time have cost us about $75,000 per year. We couldn't afford that. Or we could ask our children for help with Wilma's care but wanted to shield them from having to decide where to put Mom or Dad. Working with families as a pastor and seeing what this responsibility did to families made it clear to me that we needed to resolve this issue and not burden our children with it.

I had chosen to care for Wilma instead of having institutional care. I knew her better than anyone else and could figure things out not only by what the illness was doing to her but also by who Wilma was as a person. I learned that most of the times when there was conflict, it had some roots in Wilma's makeup.

For example, her mother was a very reserved person who masked her brilliance and power. Wilma was doing that too. Even though the ravages of Alzheimer's had destroyed much of the essence of who Wilma was, her intellect remained. I needed to keep that in mind as I was caring for her.

On the other hand, her father had a volatile temper which, by the time I knew him, was kept under control most of the time. My wife inherited that trait, and on occasion, her temper would flare in much the same way as her father's had. Knowing these tendencies meant that I would be able to cope in a better way and not just place all the blame on Alzheimer's. Institutional care is limited because of time constraints and lack of in-depth knowledge of the individual.

Learning from My Own Parents

Any doubts about a course of action were settled when I was forced to put my own parents in a nursing home. These two midwestern farm people, who had spent their lives helping others, were now unable to help themselves. The day I spent sharing my conclusions and ultimate decision with them was one of the worst days of my life.

Six months after their arrival at the nursing home, my mother had a series of small strokes that left her entirely comatose. My father and mother were in the same room, which meant there was no respite in his 24/7/365 vigil. I discussed the situation with the nursing-home staff, and they agreed to transfer my mother to a room where the other occupant was similar to my mother. Meanwhile, another man who was mobile and alert would be moved into the room with my father.

When I presented this option to my father, his response was very clear and direct. "No," he said, "I made a promise to her sixty-five years ago, and I'm not going to break it now"—referring to their marriage vow—"'til death do us part." My father had raised the bar for me.

It sealed my decision to seek a retirement community that suited our needs and fit our pocketbook. As we discussed this idea with our children, they were unanimous in saying, "Use your savings to the last penny for your care." We decided that what best suited our particular needs was to live in a life-care facility that matched our specific needs and our assets. After doing a lot of research, we settled on Shell Point in Florida. Resolving this issue and executing the plan became most important.

Covering All the Final Steps

When we found a good attorney to go over our papers, we made changes in our wills—the fifth time we did this in our married life. We chose our final resting place as well. It was a picturesque country cemetery, where both of our parents are buried. We went even further and went to a monument company and purchased a headstone.

We had frequent discussions about the final disposition of our bodies. Wilma was adamantly for cremation, while I was reluctant. However, the longer we lived in Florida and observed the increased acceptance of cremation, I gradually gave way to the idea. I even decided to follow the lead of another worker in our Shell Point workshop and made a container for our ashes. I used walnut wood, which came from the farm where I was born and had spent the first sixteen years of my life.

These decisions took place over several months and from numerous discussions. At the same time, there was urgency, because the day was coming when Wilma could no longer be part of the discussions or help with making decisions.

Closer to Full Recovery

During the last years, months, weeks, and then days of Wilma's life, a statement by one of our friends was most helpful. He said, "The truth is, Wilma is closer to full recovery than you are." As I watched her decline, I knew that full recovery really was nearer to my life partner.

Christmas 1999 was to be our last together. Our daughter, Marilyn, had come to be with us and, as I looked back, I realized that I had been so involved in Wilma's care that I had not seen how far she had deteriorated. On the other hand, the chaplain for Hospice was able to discern the situation more clearly. She advocated that I needed some respite and arranged for Wilma to be in Hope Hospice.

I agreed, and on January 2, 2000, I took my wife to Hope Hospice. I spent the next two days visiting friends in Florida, contacting Hope Hospice each evening to ask about her condition. When I called on January 4, I was told that there was a radical change, and I immediately returned. Wilma had drifted from the last stages of Alzheimer's to the final stage.

The professionals and volunteers at Hope Hospice made certain that Wilma was comfortable at all times. Rest, blessed rest, was coming after all those years of agitation and struggle. When I questioned the nurses about how long this would last, their reply was, "It is out of our hands."

I contacted each of the children, our pastor, and Wilma's family, and told them of her condition. Marilyn returned to share the final hours with us. At 7:00 A.M., on January 14, 2000, the last tether of earth was severed.

In my announcement of her death to the Shell Point friends and community I wrote, "Full recovery from Alzheimer's came to Wilma Fought on January 14, 2000."

FOR FURTHER THOUGHT...

Our journey together had begun on June 16, 1946, in a small white country church, on a Sunday afternoon. The front of the sanctuary was filled with a brilliant display of floral arrangements, created by my aunt and her friends in the local garden club. That journey of fifty-three years and seven months, ended with a beautiful floral arrangement put together by volunteers at Hospice House.

My prayer for every person facing what we faced is this: *"Oh God, when the time for departure from this earth arrives, may the hours be blessed with the powerful awareness of Your presence, because the best is yet to come. Amen."*